PETS' GUIDES

Gordon's Guide to
Caring for Your Guinea Pigs

Isabel Thomas

Raintree is an imprint of Capstone Global Library Limited, a company incorporated in England and Wales having its registered office at 7 Pilgrim Street, London, EC4V 6LB – Registered company number: 6695582

www.raintreepublishers.co.uk
myorders@raintreepublishers.co.uk

Edited by James Benefield and Brynn Baker
Designed by Cynthia Akiyoshi
Picture research by Tracy Cummins
Production by Victoria Fitzgerald
Originated by Capstone Global Library Limited
Printed and bound in China by RR Donnelley Asia

ISBN 978-1-406-28177-4

18 17 16 15 14
10 9 8 7 6 5 4 3 2 1

British Library Cataloguing in Publication Data
A full catalogue record for this book is available from the British Library.

Acknowledgements
We would like to thank the following for permission to reproduce photographs: Alamy: © blickwinkel, 26, © KARL REDSHAW, 14; Biosphoto: J.-L. Klein & M.-L. Hubert, front cover; Capstone Library: Karon Dubke, 5, 11, 21; Getty Images: kickers, 8, 13, Vstock LLC, 17, Yellow Dog Productions, 7; Glow Images: Arco Images/GmbH/Wegner, 19; Shutterstock: Monkey Business Images, 24; Superstock: Juniors, 22; Design Elements Shutterstock: iBird, Picsfive, R-studio.

We would like to thank Faye and Gary Taylor for their assistance in the preparation of this book.

Contents

Some words are shown in bold, **like this**. You can find out what they mean by looking in the glossary.

Do you want pet guinea pigs?

Squeak! I'm Gordon and this book is all about guinea pigs like me. Guinea pigs aren't really pigs, we're **rodents**. We make great pets. We are calm and friendly and love being with our favourite humans.

Before giving a home to guinea pigs, be sure you can look after us properly. We'll need food, water and a clean place to live. Plus, we need company, safe toys to play with and **vet** care if we get sick or injured.

Choosing your guinea pigs

Which type of guinea pig would suit your family? Smooth-coated guinea pigs like me have short fur. We are easy to care for! If you choose a long-haired or rough-coated guinea pig, you will need to become an expert at brushing guinea pig hair.

Animal shelters and **rescue centres** are the best places to find guinea pigs. You could also adopt guinea pigs from a good **breeder**, or buy them from a pet shop. Visit the guinea pigs first to make sure they are happy and healthy.

I get very lonely when I'm on my own. Guinea pigs like to live in small groups, so you will need to get at least two. Choose girl guinea pigs or boy guinea pigs.

If you would like to keep boy guinea pigs, it is best to get two brothers. Otherwise, the boy guinea pigs might fight! Getting all boy or all girl guinea pigs prevents unwanted baby guinea pigs.

Getting ready

Now it's time to shop for everything your new guinea pig needs. First on the list is a home big enough to run around and explore. Also make sure it's tall, so I can stand up on my back legs without bumping my head.

Fill my home with places to hide, tunnels to play in, rocks to climb and wooden toys to chew. Don't forget the bedroom! A clay flowerpot will do. I like to nibble everything, so even the bedding should be safe to eat.

Welcome home

We can live outdoors if the temperature is 15 degrees Celsius (59 degrees Fahrenheit) or warmer. If it gets colder than this where you live, keep me indoors. If I get too hot I can get very sick, so keep my cage away from sunny windows, radiators and heaters. Also, keep us away from direct sunlight.

The perfect spot for my new home is:

- quiet and calm
- protected from draughts. I like lots of space for warm bedding too!
- away from other pets. I'm scared of cats and dogs!
- always between 15–20 degrees Celsius (59–68 degrees Fahrenheit)
- somewhere I won't disturb you at night

Feeding time

I like to nibble hay and drink water all day long. Give me guinea pig pellets every morning and evening. These are made from plants, seeds and vegetables, with plenty of a special chemical called Vitamin C to keep me healthy.

Don't forget the snacks! Leafy green vegetables will make me a happy and healthy guinea pig. You can even give me fresh grass and dandelion leaves from the garden. Yum!

Handling

Spend time with me every day. At first I may freeze or hide if I'm feeling scared. Be quiet and gentle. Offer me treats, such as small pieces of a carrot or an apple, to show me that you are friendly and safe.

Pick me up safely by supporting my bottom with one hand, and hold me close to your chest. Sit down when you are handling me, so I don't get hurt if I wriggle out of your hands. Stroke me gently and I might even purr.

Playtime

Once I've settled in, please let me play outside my cage every day. Create a safe space with places to hide. Watch me carefully to make sure I don't escape or get into trouble. I like to chew everything and I don't know what is dangerous.

Put some exciting toys in my cage, so I can keep playing when you're asleep or at school. Plastic pipes and large cardboard tubes make good tunnels. Rocks and ramps are fun to climb. Deep piles of hay are great for digging.

Cleaning my home

A good guinea pig owner has jobs to do every day. Change my water and clear away any leftover pellets or fresh food. Take out any damp bedding and droppings. Once a week, give my whole cage a full cleaning.

Gordon's cleaning tips:

- clear out the dirty bedding
- scrub my cage floor with warm water and a **disinfectant**
- remember to wash my toys and hiding places, too
- let everything dry
- fill my cage with fresh, clean bedding

Grooming and tooth care

While you are busy keeping my cage clean, I'm busy **grooming** myself. Help me keep my fur clean and shiny by brushing me with a special soft brush. If you have long-haired guinea pigs, you'll need to do this every day.

Like all rodents, my teeth never stop growing.
I stop them from getting too long by **gnawing**
on wood. They don't overgrow often, but
please make sure I always have branches,
twigs or unpainted wooden toys.

Visiting the vet

Take your guinea pigs to visit a vet every year.
Go back if we get ill between check-ups.
Guinea pigs are not very good at showing
you when they're sick or injured.

Look out for these signs that I need to visit a vet:

- my teeth are getting too long
- I'm coughing, sneezing or **wheezing**
- I'm not playing or moving, or I am hiding more than usual
- I have diarrhoea or a dirty bottom
- I'm doing fewer droppings than usual
- I'm not grooming myself or my skin looks strange or lumpy
- you spot any **mites** or **worms** on my body or in my droppings
- I become thin very quickly

Holiday care

If you go on holiday, find someone to look after me while you're away. Tell them how to change my food and water, keep my cage clean, and help me exercise. Give them the list of signs I show if I need to visit a vet.

Moving can be scary for guinea pigs.
If I have to stay in a different place while
you're away, take my toys along, too. The
smell will remind me of home.

Guinea pig facts

- Guinea pigs are also called "cavies".

- Guinea pigs don't need much sleep. They eat, play and explore day and night.

- Guinea pigs make lots of different noises. They "wheek" when excited, "chutt" when exploring and "purr" when handled.

- Guinea pigs usually live for four to seven years.

Gordon's top tips

- Make my cage as large as possible, with lots of space to run around. Fill it with plenty of things to see and do.

- Don't worry if you see me eating my droppings. This is how I get all the goodness out of the food!

- You can teach guinea pigs to go to the toilet in a litter box.

- When cleaning my cage, use vinegar and an old toothbrush to get rid of crusty stains.

Glossary

animal shelter organization that cares for animals that do not have homes

breeder person who helps animals to have babies in an organized way

disinfectant chemicals used to clean and kill germs

gnaw bite or chew something again and again

groom clean an animal's fur or skin

mite tiny spider-like insect that lives on larger animals

rescue centre organization that rescues animals that are lost, injured or not being taken care of properly

rodent type of animal with front teeth that never stop growing, such as guinea pigs

vet person trained to care for ill and injured animals

wheezing breathing with a whistling or rattling sound

worm tiny animal that lives inside other animals and can make them ill

Find out more

Books

Guinea Pig (My New Pet), Jinny Johnson
(Franklin Watts, 2013)

Guinea Pigs (A Pet's Life), Anita Ganeri
(Heinemann-Raintree, 2009)

Websites

www.bluecross.org.uk/2152-2805/caring-for-your-guinea-pig.html
Learn more about caring for guinea pigs on the
Blue Cross website.

www.rspca.org.uk/allaboutanimals/pets/rodents/guineapigs
Discover more about guinea pigs from the RSPCA.

Index